W9-CCG-626

You smell like an acre of wet dogs.

I'm not saying you're old, but who else remembers when Baskin Robbins only had two flavors.

Excuse me, sir. When's the baby due?

Don't ever change. I want to forget you just the way you are.

Why don't you hop in your geekmobile and cruise for dweebettes?

By Jim Davis
Published by Ballantine Books:

GARFIELD AT LARGE
GARFIELD GAINS WEIGHT
GARFIELD BIGGER THAN LIFE
GARFIELD WEIGHS IN
GARFIELD TAKES THE CAKE
GARFIELD EATS HIS HEART OUT
GARFIELD SITS AROUND THE HOUSE
GARFIELD TIPS THE SCALES
GARFIELD LOSES HIS FEET
GARFIELD MAKES IT BIG
GARFIELD ROLLS ON
GARFIELD OUT TO LUNCH
GARFIELD'S FOOD FOR THOUGHT
GARFIELD SWALLOWS HIS PRIDE
GARFIELD WORLDWIDE
GARFIELD ROUNDS OUT
GARFIELD CHEWS THE FAT
GARFIELD GOES TO WAIST
GARFIELD HANGS OUT
GARFIELD TAKES UP SPACE
GARFIELD SAYS A MOUTHFUL
GARFIELD BY THE POUND
GARFIELD KEEPS HIS CHINS UP
GARFIELD TAKES HIS LICKS
GARFIELD HITS THE BIG TIME
GARFIELD PULLS HIS WEIGHT

GARFIELD'S BIG FAT HAIRY JOKE BOOK
GARFIELD'S INSULTS, PUT-DOWNS, & SLAMS
GARFIELD'S BIG FAT SCARY JOKE BOOK
GARFIELD'S BIG FAT HOLIDAY JOKE BOOK
GARFIELD'S SON OF BIG FAT HAIRY JOKES

Books published by The Ballantine Publishing Group
are available at quantity discounts on bulk purchases
for premium, educational, fund-raising, and special
sales use. For details, please call 1-800-733-3000.

GARFIELD'S INSULTS, PUT-DOWNS & SLAMS

Created by
Jim "Hairball" Davis

Written by
Mark "Airball" Acey
and
Jim "Cheeseball" Kraft

BALLANTINE BOOKS • NEW YORK

Sale of this book without a front cover may be unauthorized. If this book is coverless, it may have been reported to the publisher as "unsold or destroyed" and neither the author nor the publisher may have received payment for it.

A Ballantine Book
Published by The Ballantine Publishing Group
Copyright © 1994 by United Feature Syndicate, Inc.

All rights reserved under International and Pan-American Copyright Conventions. Published in the United States by The Ballantine Publishing Group, a division of Random House, Inc., New York, and simultaneously in Canada by Random House of Canada Limited, Toronto.

Ballantine and colophon are registered trademarks of Random House, Inc.

www.randomhouse.com/BB/

Library of Congress Catalog Card Number: 93-90861

ISBN 0-345-38689-2

Printed in Canada

First Ballantine Books Edition: April 1994

15   14

CATS HAVE A ROUGH TONGUE

AND THEY'RE NOT AFRAID TO USE IT

CONTENTS

INTRODUCTION	1
BODY SLAMS	3
DRESSED TO KILL ... or at least NAUSEATE!	27
COMICAL CURSES	35
SNAPPY COMEBACKS	41
NERD IS THE WORD	55
CAREER JEERS	63
DUMB AS AN ODIE	73
OUT TO LUNCH	83
DARTS TO THE HEART	87
ALLITERATIVE AFFRONTS	97
COTTON-PICKIN' PUT-DOWNS	101
HIGHBROW BROWBEATING	107
PUTTING DOWN THE DOG	111
BIRTHDAY BASHING	119
NONVERBAL JABS	125
LIFE IN THE FAT LANE	133
PARTING SHOTS	143

INTRODUCTION

Obviously, I need no introduction. That would be an insult to your intelligence. (Hey, your lips are moving.)

No, I'm here to arm you with an arsenal of insults, wisecracks, and surefire comebacks. In a battle of wits, it helps to have lots of ammunition. Of course, insults don't always have to be lethal weapons. Often they merely take the form of playful banter—like a water balloon tossed back and forth between friends.

So whether you want to snub a snob, bust a bully, or just diss a dopey dog (a personal favorite), this book contains enough comic firepower to launch a full-scale offensive.

Well, what are you waiting for—an invitation? Turn the page, Molasses Brain, and let's get cooking. I'm starving for some laughs.

BODY SLAMS

*What's that strange growth on
your neck? Oh, it's your head!*

Everybody slams somebody sometime. And many of these verbal blows are directed to the body. Know what I mean, Muttonhead?

These slaps in the face often take two forms. They can be zingers designed to get under a person's skin, or they can simply be funny names utilizing parts of the body. This latter approach is especially enjoyable as it affords a great chance to be creative. Sure, there are plenty of "real" insulting names that any lamebrain can find in a dictionary (so I had Jon find you some; see below). But the real fun comes from creating your own moronic monikers. All you have to do is slap a funny word in front of a body part. Know what I mean, Carp Face?

Traditionally, "head," "face," and "brain" have worked best. But for the sake of nonsense, I've thrown in—at no extra charge—lists of silly words and offbeat body parts. Now all you need to do is mix and match. Just think of it as your starter kit. So, are you ready to get goofy, Armadillo Lips? Let the bashing and tongue-lashing begin!

READY-MADE NAMES

airhead

bonehead

blockhead

pinhead

lunkhead

cheesehead

chowderhead

knucklehead

chucklehead

dunderhead

hammerhead

egghead

fathead

deadhead

birdbrain

harebrain

blabbermouth

numskull

MIX 'N' MATCH

Just match a word from column "Diss" with a word from column "This." Think you can handle that, Gnat Brain?

6

"Diss"	*"This"*
moose	back
drool	neck
bubble	head
pork	nose
platypus	lips
hairball	ankles
corndog	brain
zit	face
zipper	puss
possum	mug
blubber	ears
burp	mouth
rutabaga	spleen
munchkin	jowls
puke	gums
cheese	nostrils
raisin	belly
wombat	bladder
snot	eyes
jumbo	gut
banana	liver
meatball	skull
aardvark	spine
phlegm	tongue
iguana	toes
pygmy	rump
pus	teeth
inflato-	snout
goat	glands
tick	butt
fur	fingers

"Diss"	*"This"*
scab	noggin
newt	earlobes
yak	knees
tuna	skin
tuba	bones
booger	hair
salami	jaw
sheep-dip	pelvis
weasel	pancreas
slime	scalp
baboon	
maggot	
lard	
chutney	

BODY SHOTS
Verbal blows from the head to the toes

Today's lesson is gross anatomy

Head

Is that your head or a hotel for lice?

You have the perfect head . . . for a totem pole!

You have a pretty little head. For a head, it's pretty little!

I've seen nicer heads on a witch doctor's belt!

Last time I saw a noggin like yours was on Mr. Potato Head!

Hey, Chrome Dome! Is that your head or a bloated cue ball?

The only thing smooth about you is your scalp.

Hey, Cone Head! Mind if I play ring toss?

I've seen nicer heads in a cabbage patch.

How can such a humongous head hold such a puny brain?

Your head's so big, if you were a cowboy, you'd have to wear a *twenty*-gallon hat!

You should be a bone doctor. You've got the head for it!

Heard you had your head examined, but they couldn't find anything.

You're like Odie. You've got a soft heart . . . and a head to match!

Is that your head, or is there a fungus growing on your
  neck?

Hair

Nice hair. Still styling it with a weed-whacker?
I've seen better looking hair in the shower drain.
I've seen nicer hair coming out of my grandma's nose.
Is that your hair, or is something nesting on your
  head?
Your hairdo really suits your face. They're *both* ugly.
I'm not saying your hair is bad, but my cat coughs up
  better looking stuff.
Why don't you put your hair on a leash where it be-
  longs?
Why don't you do something different with your hair?
  Like, wash it.
People who think there's an oil shortage have never
  seen your hair.
What shampoo do you use? Pennzoil or Quaker State?
Your hair has so much mousse in it, you could sprout
  antlers!
Your hair's so greasy, you could fry chicken in it!

You're lucky. If your bike needs oil, you can just rub
   your hair on it.
Nice hair. Did you butcher it yourself?
Is your hair always like that, or did you just electrocute
   yourself?
Excuse me. Are you related to Don King?
Who does your hair? I want to know who to avoid.
Nice hairdo. But isn't it early for Halloween?
You'd look better with long hair. Especially if you
   combed it down over your face.

Face

Know what goes best with a face like yours? A paper
   bag.
You've got a face only a mother gorilla could love.
Is that your face, or did your neck throw up?
Your face reminds me of a famous TV star ... Lassie!
You're not ugly. You're just facially challenged.
It's strange to see a face like yours without eight legs
   attached.
Be it ever so homely, there's no face like yours.
I've seen gargoyles with nicer faces.
If I had your face, I'd save up for a nicer one.

You have a face only a plastic surgeon could love!

A face like yours doesn't come along every day. Just every full moon!

Is that your face or a zit with teeth?

Hey, Pizza Face! Is that a pimple or a volcano?

If that zit erupts, it could wipe out the city!

I thought craters that big were only found on the moon!

Hey, Peach-Fuzz Face! You gonna shave or just pluck?

A face like yours belongs in the movies ... horror movies!

Know what I like about your face? Me neither.

You have a striking face. So who's been striking it?

Is that your face, or did your pants fall down?

Your face is like a work of modern art. You can't tell what it is.

You have the perfect face ... for a dart board!

You're two-faced. And they're *both* ugly!

Is that a mustache, or did a woolly worm just crawl out of your nose?

Nice whiskers. For a broom!

I'm not going to say mean things about your looks. Your face speaks for itself.

Who did your make-up? Bozo?

With a face like yours, *every* day is Halloween!

Is that your nose, or did someone park a blimp on your face?

Your nose is so big you should rent it out for dances!

Don't look up! Your big nose might poke a hole in the ozone layer!

Compared to you, Pinocchio was snub-nosed!

Last time I saw a nose like yours it had an elephant attached to it!

Hey, Hose Nose! Can you pick up a peanut with that thing?

If it starts raining, can I stand under your nose to keep dry?

Nice nose. Does it come with a ski lift?

Last time I saw a snout like yours was on a porpoise.

Are those nostrils or airplane hangars?

Don't inhale. A schnozz like yours could suck all the oxygen out of the room!

I've seen a nose like yours before, but it looked better on the baboon.

Don't turn your head too fast. You might bludgeon someone with your nose.

The great thing about your nose is that you'll always have a place to hang your coat.

The only thing grosser than your nose is what's inside it.

Is that your nose, or did a booger petrify on your face?

Last time I saw a honker like yours was on a hot dog bun!

You've got a nose for business. I mean, you could use it as a billboard.

Is that your nose, or are you trying to snort a banana?

With a snout like yours, who needs anteaters?

Up your nose with ...

> ... my stinky toes!
> ... a fire hose!
> ... a flock of crows!
> ... Axl Rose!
> ... my wet gym clothes!

Ears

Your ears aren't big ... for a basset hound!

If I had your ears, I'd wire them up and make satellite dishes!

With ears like yours, you could hear a pin drop on the moon!

Some people get water in their ears, but yours could hold a whole pool!

You've got ears like a famous movie star ... Mickey Mouse!

Hey, Dumbo! Why don't you flap your ears and fly away?

Nice ears. How come you didn't get the tusks to go with them?

Can you swat flies with those suckers?

Are those your ears, or did two flying saucers just crash into the sides of your head?

I'm not saying your ears are big, but you could wear earrings made by Michelin!

It's great to have ears like yours. You can go hang gliding without a glider!

Your ears are so big, they had to pierce them with a harpoon!

Your ears are so big, you don't wear ear muffs. You wear ear parkas!

Never clean your ears with a Q-Tip. Always use a mop!

Nice ears ... for a Vulcan.

If Van Gogh had ears like yours, he would've cut them *both* off!

I've heard of boxers with "cauliflower ears," but your ears look more like deformed pumpkins!

You've got enough wax in your ears to start your own candle company!

In your ear with ...

> ... an asparagus spear!
> ... a chandelier!
> ... a longhorn steer!
> ... a tick-ridden deer!

Your mouth's so big, you could park a school bus in it!

Your mouth's so cavernous, people go spelunking in there!

I've seen rivers with smaller mouths.

You've got a yap the size of a yak.

Is that your mouth or the Grand Canyon?

Your mouth's so big, you can eat a foot-long hot dog sideways.

Your mouth's so big, it takes you an hour to put on your lipstick.

Your mouth's the perfect size ... for your foot.

Your mouth's like a convenience store ... open twenty-four hours a day.

Hey, Motor Mouth! Kill your engine!

Your mouth oughta come with a mute button!

Hey, Gym Locker Breath! Ever hear of gargling?

Your breath's so bad, you need a Tic Tac the size of a watermelon!

Your breath smells like you gargled with "Eau d'Odie."

Is that your breath, or did you swallow Jon's sweatsocks?

Stop air pollution. Keep your mouth shut!

16

The only thing that smells worse than your feet is your breath.

Hey, Mildew Mouth! Your breath could stun a moose.

Teeth

Nice teeth ... for a beaver!

I've seen nicer teeth in my comb.

Are those your teeth or a coal mine?

You don't need to brush your teeth. You need to sand-blast them!

You have so many cavities there's an echo when you talk.

Is it true you brush your teeth once a year whether they need it or not?

It's neat the way that yellow sweater matches your teeth.

Is today St. Patrick's Day, or are your teeth always that green?

Those braces are really attractive. To a magnet!

Hey, Tin Grin! Set off any metal detectors lately?

Are those braces, or are your teeth under arrest?

Hey, Metal Mouth! Don't look now, but there are railroad tracks on your teeth!

17

You go to a dentist twice a year ... once for each
  tooth.
Your teeth are like pearls. Really scarce.
Are you going to eat that apple, or gum it to death?
You'd look good with a gold tooth. In fact, you'd look
  good with *any* teeth!
You have such nice clean teeth. At least they look that
  way in the jar.

Stomach

These piggish put-downs were threatening to eat up all
the space in this section, so I gave them their own
chunky chapter later in the book (see "Life in the Fat
Lane").

Is it storming out, or is that just your thunder thighs clapping together?

Some people look good in shorts. Then there's you.

I'm not saying you have fat legs, but who else wears industrial-strength pantyhose?

The world hasn't seen legs like yours since the brontosaurus died out!

You've got calves only a cow could love.

Don't look now, but somebody put toothpicks where your legs should be!

Legs like yours are great on camping trips. You can always rub them together to start a fire.

Nice legs . . . for a flamingo.

Your legs look like a turkey's on the day after Thanksgiving.

I've seen better looking legs on a centipede!

Nice gams. Maybe next time you can get some with muscles.

You're so bowlegged, a truck could drive through there.

I've seen tables with nicer legs than yours.

Your feet are so big, when you dance, you step on *everybody's* toes!

Your feet are so large, Bigfoot could wear your baby shoes!

If your feet were any bigger, they'd need license plates.

Your feet are so big, you could get a job helping Smokey the Bear stamp out forest fires!

I'm not saying your feet are big, but who else wears Paul Bunyan brand gym shoes?

If your feet were any bigger, they'd be yards!

You've got feet only a clown could love!

Are those toenails or talons?

Your feet smell so bad, your shoes are gagging.

Is there a dead skunk nearby, or did you just take off your shoes?

Your feet don't stink. And Odie's not stupid!

I think you stepped on something smelly. Like your feet!

Want to fight air pollution? Then keep your shoes on.

Your feet could out-stink a gym locker!

Your feet are so stinky, you should be charged with sock abuse!

I heard you went barefoot in the park and the stink killed all the trees!

THE LONG AND THE SHORT OF IT

Too Tall

Don't think of yourself as tall. Think of yourself as a freak of nature.

Hey, Lurch! Where's the rest of the family?

You look like a flagpole with hair.

Do you eat regular food, or just nibble leaves from the treetops?

With your height, you'd make a great model. For a silo.

I'm glad you're tall. It gives me more of you to dislike.

Why don't you go hold up some telephone wires?

Banged your head on any good doorways lately?

Don't be self-conscious about your height. Save it for your face.

I could sit here all day, watching the clouds float through your head.

I promise not to ask you, "How's the weather up there?" So, how's the air traffic up there?

If you're so tall, why aren't you in the NBA?
Your extra height will be great for stocking that top shelf at the grocery store.
You're more than a tall person. You're also dumb.
You don't slouch much ... for a tall person.
Do you play basketball, or is your height just a big waste?
Nice height. Too bad it didn't come with coordination.

Low blows

You're so short, you have to duck under dogs.
Why don't you go play in the cottage with the other dwarfs?
You'd need a growth spurt just to be short.
How's everything in Munchkin Land?
You look taller on the Lucky Charms box.
Need a ride, Half-Pint? Hop in the glove compartment.
You're so short, you can't see over the carpet.
You're so short, even your jockey shorts are too long.
You're so short, you need a ladder to reach the curb.
Everyone looks up to someone, but *you* look up to everyone.
I promise not to make fun of your height. I would never stoop to that.

What's your favorite dessert ... shortcake?

If you were any shorter, you could date Barbie.

I used to be your height ... when I was *two*!

Call the cops! Somebody stole your height!

You're small now, but someday you'll grow up to be short.

I don't think you're a shrimp. I think you're more like an amoeba.

I have socks taller than you.

I scrape runts like you off my shoes.

Get taller or get lost!

You shouldn't be so short. It's bad for your height.

Congratulations! I hear you were offered a job modeling for fire hydrants.

You're short. You're ugly. You're Runtzilla!

Hey, Peewee! Why don't you suck fertilizer and grow?

You're so puny, you couldn't beat an egg.

I'd call you short to your face, but I can't bend down that far.

People come in every size. Too bad *you* only come in pint-size.

Look! It's a mini-kid!

Hey, Pygmy Face! Couldn't your parents afford a full-size kid?

I apologize for the "short" jokes. Please don't punch me in the ankle.

Lookin' bad

And I don't mean good

I don't know where you got your looks, but I hope you
   kept the receipt.

Appearances can be deceiving. Or in your case, disgusting.

You were such an ugly baby, your mom didn't keep
   you in a playpen. She kept you in a pigpen.

Women like your body. They like it to go away.

Maybe you should become a goalie. You'd look better
   wearing a hockey mask.

Know what I like about your looks? Nothing!

With your looks, you could win a prize ... at a dog
   show!

It's okay to be ugly, but you're overdoing it.

You were such an ugly baby, even politicians wouldn't
   kiss you!

The last time I saw something that looked like you, I
   flushed it!

You look really good ... for roadkill.

Can I have your picture? I want to scare my sister.

Your pictures don't do you justice. They look just like
   you!

Sit down and take a mess off your feet.

You'd look better with your glasses off. Actually, you'd look best with *my* glasses off.

Know what goes great with a body like yours? A barf bag.

You're so ugly, when you look in the mirror, your reflection throws up!

Looks aren't everything. And in your case, they're nothing.

Your looks aren't half-bad. They're *all* bad!

"Beauty is skin deep, but ugly goes clear to the bone"

TOP TEN PROCEDURES GARFIELD WOULD PERFORM IF HE WERE A PLASTIC SURGEON

10. Hair weave: Ziggy
 9. Tongue tuck: Odie
 8. Liposuction: Porky Pig
 7. Skin bleaching: The Hulk
 6. Ear snip: Mr. Spock
 5. Beak job: Opus
 4. Electrolysis: ALF
 3. Dermabrasion: Ninja Turtles
 2. Breast implants: Olive Oyl
 1. Humpectomy: Quasimodo

DRESSED TO KILL

. . . or at least NAUSEATE!

Clothes make the man. And sometimes they make the man look stupid: Boy George, Liberace, any guy in a kilt. Personally, I prefer fur. It's always in style—at least for us animals. But enough about me and my impeccable wardrobe. Let's taunt the terminally fashion-impaired:

I heard you gave your clothes to charity and they gave them back!

Words can't describe your outfit, so I'll just throw up!

Your clothes always attract attention. Not to mention flies.

You must shop at fine dumpsters everywhere.

Nice dress. How many potatoes did it hold?

That's a killer coat. It kills me to look at it.

Your clothes are so drab, they look like they escaped from a prison laundry!

You have a style all your own. And I hope it s not catching!

I see you're wearing an outfit by your favorite designer
... Clearance.

Love your sweater. Does the bag lady know you bor-
rowed it?

Where'd you buy those pants? J. C. Ugly?

You look like the cover girl for *Scuzmopolitan*.

If I were in your shoes, I'd polish them.

Your clothes make a statement. Too bad that statement
is "I have no taste."

I hear the "Fashion Police" have an APB out on your
wardrobe.

Those pants fit you like a glove ... a baseball glove.

Nice blouse. I wonder if it'll ever come back in style.

Your clothes look good considering the shape they're
on.

Your swimsuit is becoming ... becoming too small for
that gut.

Everybody looks bad sometimes, but not you. You
look bad *all* the time.

That hat is so lame you should shoot it!

That bathrobe is so ratty it belongs in the sewer.

Your clothes are so worn, they look like they came
from a *third*-hand store!

I see you're into "grunge." I can also smell it.

I had a shirt just like that after the dog threw up on it.

Nice tie. Those stains just add to the design.

Your outfit is in a clash by itself.

Nice look ... for a court jester!

Those socks are louder than Binky with a bullhorn!

That shirt's so loud it should come with a muffler!

If your tie were any louder, my ears would bleed!

I've seen better looking shoes on a horse.

Know what would go great with your suit? A blackout!

Nice duds. Your mom buy those for ya?

I don't want to rag on your rags, but I've seen nicer
clothes on a scarecrow.

You're a real clotheshorse. When you put on your
clothes, you look like a horse.

The only thing worse than what you're wearing is the
body that's wearing it!

Did you make that outfit yourself, or is someone else
to blame?

You don't need a garment bag for those clothes. You
need a *garbage* bag.

Nice shoes. Was Bozo World having a sale?

Your shoes are so ugly they hurt *my* feet!

Some people look bad in clothes like that—and you're
one of them.

Where'd you get that shirt? I'll be sure not to shop there.

Your clothes may be ugly, but they're you.

How many polyesters were killed to make that suit?

Are all your cool clothes in the wash?

Those jeans are awfully baggy, but you'll spread into them.

I like your reversible jacket. Now if only it came with a reversible face ...

Your feet must smell, 'cause those shoes stink.

Your clothes will be back in style any day now.

Call the "Fashion Squad." Your clothes need emergency assistance.

TOP TEN PLACES JON BUYS HIS CLOTHES

10. Al's A-1 Exhumed Suits
 9. Ray's Tub o' Ties
 8. The Fashion Blemish
 7. Jiffy Pants
 6. Elton John's Funwear For Fellas
 5. The Guy Sty
 4. Big Wally's Garage Sale Seconds
 3. The Clown Outlet
 2. Mr. Tacky's
 1. Geeks R Us

TOP TEN ATROCITIES IN JON'S WARDROBE

10. Lime leisure suit
9. Polka-dot sweatsocks
8. Squirting bow tie
7. One of those goofy hats Goober wears
6. Tap shoes
5. Hand-me-down knickers
4. Plaid underwear
3. Kraut-stained lederhosen
2. Coonskin cap
1. Tutu

COMICAL CURSES

May you laugh till your head explodes!

No, not those kinds of curses, you #$@*%! (Any nit-wit can be foul; it takes a true wit to be funny.) I'm talking *kooky* curses, the kind of mischief and mayhem that a wacked-out witch might brew up. And if you still don't get it, then "May you be mooned by a portly baboon!"

May you floss a pit bull!
May your tongue grow fur!
May all your relatives move in with you—*permanently*!
May you spend prom night organizing your sock drawer!
May you be trapped in a phone booth with an incontinent hippo!
May you, Kermit, and Miss Piggy become embroiled in a deadly love triangle!
May your TV only get the weather channel!
May you uncork a burp registering 6.2 on the Richter scale!
May you wake up with a disgruntled buffalo on your face!
May your hair hurt!
May huge weeds grow in your belly button!

May you go snorkeling in a pool of dog drool!

May a family of squirrels build a nest inside your head!

May you jump for joy ... into an open manhole!

May you be grounded until you turn forty!

May demons repossess your car!

May you suck melons through the gap in your teeth!

May you find an antler in your chocolate mousse!

May a sweaty sumo wrestler get stuck in your bathtub!

May you pick your nose on national TV!

May you meet a huge spider with an attitude!

May the raisins in your cereal sprout wings!

May you step in a cow pie wearing your new Air Jordans!

May you have "morning breath" twenty-fours hours a day!

May you give mouth-to-snout resuscitation to a hog with halitosis!

May your cat food bill surpass the national debt!

May mutant leftovers breed in your refrigerator!

May deranged monks enslave you in a grape-stomping chain gang!

May you scale Mt. Rushmore, then fall off Lincoln's nose!

May you be kept up all night by a yodeling parrot!

May you be trapped for a week in a health food store!

May your blind date have a Klingon forehead and Ferengi ears!

May your bunions smell like onions!

May you look worse than your driver's license photo!

May you blow your life savings on bogus hair tonics!

May your cat sharpen his claws on your waterbed!

May you scrape the tartar from Odie's teeth ... with *your* teeth!

May voracious boll weevils munch holes in your undies!

May your Miracle Ear go dead during game seven of the World Series!

May a runaway hubcap from a speeding car lodge itself up your nose!

May a psychotic beaver gnaw off your wooden leg!

May you spend your honeymoon at a monster truck rally!

May your firstborn be named Arbuckle!

May you spontaneously combust!

SNAPPY COMEBACKS

I refuse to have a battle of wits with an unarmed person

Unless you want to stay stuck in the "I'm rubber, you're glue . . ." stage of repartee, you'll need to sharpen your wits. Watch and learn from the master blaster. (Hey, I'm quick-witted and the first to admit it!)

Are you hip to the quip? Then fill in the thought balloon with your favorite wicked retort from the choices below:

Garfield: With the bearded lady or the alligator girl?
             Quick! Somebody call Ripley's!
             Yeah right. And my diet begins tomorrow.

And I saw Elvis kissing Santa Claus!

With a fashion consultant, I hope.

Within your own species?

Yeah, and Odie just joined Mensa.

And I just won ten million dollars in the Clearinghouse Sweepstakes.

Give my regards to your mom.

Oh, did she escape from the asylum?

Must be a blue moon.

Not to mention an infinite capacity for self-delusion.

I REALLY THINK YOU SHOULD DIET THIS WEEK

Garfield: And I really think you should jump naked into a pool of piranhas!

Think again, Bran Brain!

Then your think tank must be leaking.

And I think you have a death wish.

I can't diet for medical reasons. It makes me hungry.

Sorry, I only diet between meals.

I would, but our ignored desserts might develop low self-esteem.

Haven't you heard? Rice cakes cause mange.

I'll diet when you get a date.

Cruelty, thy name is Jon.

Have I ever mentioned that I'm a deranged postal employee?

Garfield: More than what?

I would, but I can't afford the shoes.

And you should gargle more.

Why? I'm the perfect weight for my shape.

Exercise is for the loafing-impaired.

I'll join a gym when they put in a dessert bar.

Okay, I'll exercise my right not to exercise.

I prefer lay-downs to sit-ups.

You're right. I'll start with a brisk nap.

Sorry, but I don't believe in self-abuse.

I believe in conserving energy—especially my own.

If we were meant to sweat, we'd have been born with sweatbands!

Garfield: Years of hard work.
Practice! Practice! Practice!
I'm not lazy. I'm motivationally deficient.
Some call it laziness. I call it deep thought.
It's a gift!
Born lucky, I guess.
I'd tell you, but I'm too lazy.
How did you get to be so nerdy, Jon?

Did you do your homework?
No, the dog did it for me.
No, the TV wouldn't let me.
No, I'm trying to kick the habit.
No, I did some other kid's homework.
No, I like being ignorant.

How was school today?
It was school-ish.
A living hell, like always.
How should I know? I spent the day in Vegas.
The police will fill you in.
Not bad. It only scarred me for life.

Did you bring your lunch?

No, I'm going to eat yours.

No, I just carry this brown bag because it looks cool.

I'm not sure. I'll look in my lunch bag.

No, it brought me.

No, I'll just regurgitate yesterday's and eat it again.

Are you going out dressed like that?

No, I'm going to strip before I go out the door.

Yes, all my geeky clothes are in the wash.

Are you staying in dressed like *that*?

I have to. It's a law.

Yes. Unless you like what I'm wearing.

Are you gonna eat that?

No, I'm gonna have it bronzed and put on my mantle.

Only if you want it.

No, I'm gonna keep it in my locker until it mutates.

No, I'm gonna teach it to do tricks.

Yes, but I'd rather stick it up your nose.

Is that a new shirt?

No, I just got a new chest.

It was when I bought it.

No, these are pants. I just wear them funny.

It'd better be, or I'm never shopping at that store again!

Yes. Some of us can afford new clothes.

Did you get a haircut?

No, I got them all cut.

No, I put my hair in the dryer, and it shrank.

I had to. I was starting to look like *you*!

No, I had my head enlarged.
No, it's a tonsorial illusion.

Where are your manners?
I left them in my locker.
I dunno. I thought *you* had them.
When I was ten, they ran away from home.
I gave them the day off.
I belched them into the next county.

If all the other kids jump off a bridge, are you going to?
That depends. Will it mess up my hair?
Sure. Maybe I'll land on a fat kid.
As long as the line's not too long.
No, I'd rather jump off a building.
I think you can do that at Disneyworld.

Are you deaf?
I wasn't until you started yelling.
Sorry, I can't read lips.
What? I can't hear you!
Yes. My ears close whenever your mouth opens.
No, but I'm willing to learn.

How many times do I have to tell you this?
Don't stop now—you're getting close to the record!
If I guess the right number, do I get a prize?
I can't tell without a calculator.
Two hundred and fifty, give or take a million.
I don't know. We haven't studied that in math class.

Why can't you be more like your brother?
Just lucky, I guess.
I tried, but his clothes don't fit me.
Sorry, I'm not into geekiness.
Hasn't our family suffered enough already?
I'd rather be more like the dog.

Didn't I tell you to clean up this mess?
No habla anglais.
You must have me confused with someone from a parallel universe.
Have I told you how nice you look today?
Didn't the courts outlaw cruel and unusual punishment?
I did, but my evil twin messed it up again.

It's time to get up!
I just got up yesterday.
Tell morning to come back later.
I'll rise, but I won't shine.
I just need five more hours.
Call my school. Tell them I died.

"Think I should let my hair grow?"
"Yeah, preferably over your face."

"I feel fit as a fiddle."
"But you look more like a tuba."

"I admit it. It was my fault."
"That's okay. You're only subhuman."

"Have I shown you my vacation pictures?"
"No, and I appreciate it."

"I'd have to be a doofus to lend you money."
"Cool. Gimme five bucks."

"What's this stupid painting supposed to be?"
"It's an abstract representation of your mother."

"You're spoiled rotten."
"No, I'm not. That's your own B.O. you're smelling."

"I'm so hungry I could eat a horse."
"You look like you could eat a whole team."

"I'd go to the ends of the earth for you."
"Yeah, but would you stay there?"

"I'm nobody's fool."
"Well, maybe someone will adopt you."

"I read your letter. Who wrote it for you?"
"Who read it to you?"

'Know what I'm going to be when I graduate?"
"A senior citizen?"

50

"Traveling has broadened my horizons."
"Not to mention your waistline."

"I'm not myself today."
"Yeah, I've noticed the improvement."

"You're an imbecile!"
"I know you are, but what am I?"

"I just came from the beauty parlor."
"Too bad they were closed."

"I've never played that badly before."
"What, you mean you've actually played before?"

"I'm gonna give you a piece of my mind."
"Are you sure you can afford it?"

"You're pretty dirty."
"I know. And I'm even prettier when I'm clean."

"Why did you put a worm in your sister's bed?"
"I couldn't find an iguana."

"I'm a sound sleeper."
"Yeah, you sound like a jackhammer."

"How do you like my outfit?"
"Please, not while I'm eating."

"Lend me a quarter. I want to call a friend."
"Here's fifty cents. Call them both."

"Do you say a prayer before you eat?"
"We don't have to. *My* mom's a good cook."

"I have an open mind."
"Well, it oughta be closed for repairs."

"You're the ugliest person I ever saw."
"Guess you've never looked in the mirror."

"I'll have you know you can't sleep in my class."
"I could if you'd talk a little softer."

"Success hasn't gone to my head."
"No, just to your mouth."

"I've changed my mind."
"Well, it can't be any worse than your old one."

"Nobody makes a fool of me."
"Yeah, you can do that all by yourself."

Last, but certainly not least, there's the snappiest comeback of them all, the all-purpose "Big Fat Hairy Deal." You can't go wrong with this gem. But you've got to say it right:

TOP TEN INCORRECT WAYS OF SAYING "BIG FAT HAIRY DEAL"

10. "Big fat hairy duck"
 9. "Big fat dickory dock"
 8. "Land o' goshen"
 7. "Big fit happy seal"
 6. "Big fat ferris wheel"
 5. "Large obese hirsute agreement"
 4. "Makes me no nevermind"
 3. "Big fat cherry peel!"
 2. "Big fat furry veal"
 1. "So what?"

NERD IS THE WORD

Can you say 'Arbuckle'?

Clearly, Jon is the last word in nerds. His life—if you can call it that—is so boring he looks forward to dental appointments. His idea of excitement is counting the number of dimples on a golf ball. His wardrobe is right out of *GQ—Geek's Quarterly*. He's such a dweeb, he can't even get a goodnight kiss from his mom. If he were a cow, he'd be an udder failure.

Unfortunately, Jon is just the tip of the geekberg. His nerdy brethren have infiltrated our midst and are plotting to take over our planet! **BEWARE!** Contact with these creatures can be deadly (they'll bore you to death!). Should you have a close encounter of the nerd kind, proceed with derision. Remember, keep your shields up and your tongues set on "stun":

You're so nerdy, you wear a pocket protector in the shower.

57

Were you born geeky, or did your parents make you take lessons?

You're no ordinary geek. You're Geekzilla!

Hey, I hear you made the cover of *Dorks Illustrated*!

You're really attractive. In fact, you're a major dweeb magnet.

You're so wimpy, you have little bears on your underwear.

Hey, Nerdling! Why don't you go look for Waldo?

You're as interesting as a documentary on dirt.

You're as exciting as a comatose mortician.

Talk to me. I could use the sleep.

Feel free to bore me *ad nerdeum*.

Sure, I'm listening. Can't you see me yawning?

In those geeky clothes, you look almost lifelike.

Who designed your outfit? Christian Diork?

Hey, Nerdnik! If your pants were any higher, they'd reach your armpits!

What's your deal? Are you some kind of Urkel wannabe?

Don't you have some place to go? Like maybe a Barry Manilow concert.

Go play an accordion, Nerdinsky!

Why don't you hop in your geekmobile and cruise for dweebettes?

Nice wheels . . . for a demolition derby.

You are what you drive. And you're a beige station wagon.

You make a perfect couple. Kinda like the Duke and Duchess of Dork.

Hey, Goober! Go play with your stamp collection!

You could be the main attraction at Geeky World.

Hey, Loser! How's life mistreatin' you?

You're a total zero. In fact, you might even be a minus one.

I heard you talked to your plants and they died of boredom.

Next time you're out shopping, buy yourself a personality.

Go tape your glasses, Geekazoid!

Go sharpen your pencils, Nerdball!

Congratulations! I see you're finally using the grown-up scissors.

You're not nerdy. Lots of people carry around staplers.

Go kiss a computer, Technoweenie!

Hey, Gorkmeister! Eat my data!

Yo, Chiphead! Compute *this*!

Megabyte me, Digithead!

I'm not saying you're a nerd. Why state the obvious?

You're such a wuss, you get seasick taking a bubble bath.

Twits like you have their place. And it's not at *my* place!

You look like a visitor from the planet Geeko.

Nerd alert! Geekoid off the starboard bow!

Are you human or some sort of cybernerd?

It must give you a great sense of power, knowing you could bore the world to death.

You're like a breath of stale air.

You're so nerdy I could yawn.

You only bore me on days ending in *y*.

I thought this was a fun place, but you're here.

Hey, Nerdo! Gotten a life lately?

See you later, Dorkinator!

TOP TEN MOST LIKELY MEANINGS FOR THE NAME "ARBUCKLE"

10. "Wiener-chested"
 9. "Rash giver"
 8. "Pudding-brained"
 7. "Man of socks"
 6. "Dances with cows"
 5. "He who giggles in battle"
 4. "Uh-oh, here he comes"
 3. "Royal bore"
 2. "Village dweeb"
 1. "Cat-whipped"

TOP TEN LEAST LIKELY NICKNAMES FOR JON

10. Neon Jon
 9. Jon of Arabia
 8. The Gene Pool of Cool
 7. The Godson of Soul
 6. Jon the Baptist
 5. Stud Monkey
 4. Air Arbuckle
 3. The Love Doctor
 2. Genghis Jon
 1. Jon Juan

CAREER JEERS

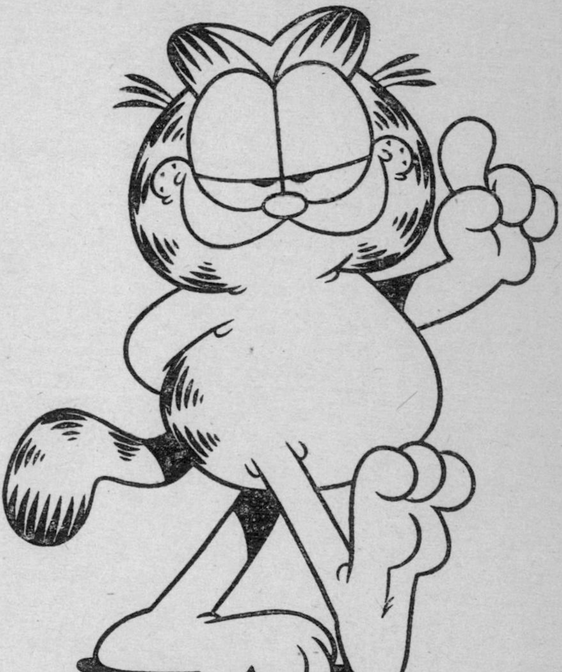

A jab for every job

It's not your job to be a snob. (That's what cats are for.) Still, should you ever wish to lampoon someone's livelihood, here are some occupational put-downs that sling mud on virtually every walk of life. Just watch your step. (By the way, you couldn't pay *me* to work.)

Teachers: "I wish *I* only had to work nine months out of the year."

Bankers: "Foreclosed on any widows or orphans lately?"

Lawyers: "Law is certainly a viable career ... if you can't get into med school."

Meteorologists: "How's the weather? As if you knew."

Morticians: "It's so comforting, the way you put a price on the loss of a loved one."

Artists: "Society needs artists. I mean, those bare walls would be sooo tiresome."

Zookeepers: "I'm sure those animals are *much* happier in captivity."

Waitpersons: "Years from now, this job will seem a lot less demeaning."

Veterinarians: "At least when you screw up, it's only on some dumb animal."

Dentists: "Aren't dentist and sadist the same thing?"

Dancers: "Lots of kids take dance lessons. Guess you never grew out of it."

Firefighters: "Bet you were one of those kids who loved to play with matches."

Clowns: "If I had your job, I wo[...]
face either."

Exterminators: "When you were a k[...]
pull the wings off flies?"

Actors: I could never do what you do[...]
well-adjusted."

Actors (TV): "Did you do any real acting b[...]
got into television?"

Politicians: "Does your mother know what you[...]
a living?"

Doctors: "You do such important work, even if you[...]
feed on the suffering of others."

Debutantes: "You're so lucky. With your name and
money you'll never have to worry about your looks."

Accountants: "I used to have an accountant. Then I
got a calculator."

Writers: "It's amazing how you can fill up all those
pages."

Secretaries: "Hey, how about getting me some coffee?"

Ad execs: "Eliminating bad breath is every bit as important as wiping out hunger and disease."

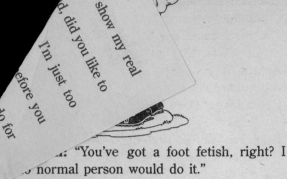

extend your adolescence

...uldn't show my real

...d, did you like to

I'm just too

...efore you

...do for

...do

...: "You've got a foot fetish, right? I
...u normal person would do it."

...workers: "Don't worry. Many people work on an
assembly line and go on to lead normal lives."

Car salesmen: "Are you between honest jobs?"

Photographers: "With the sophisticated cameras they
have now, anybody can take a great picture."

Singers: "There's no way to ruin great songs like
that."

Psychiatrists: "Didn't you graduate from Psychotic
State?"

Vice-presidents: "It must beat working for a living."

Plumbers: "Every time I flush I'm reminded of you."

Producers: "If you can't have talent, at least you can be around it."

Librarians: "Dusting those books must take a lot of training."

Mechanics: "It's amazing how much of the grease you're able to wash off."

Farmers: "How's the dirt business?"

Cab drivers: "I can see how driving a cab would make you an authority on everything."

Cartoonists: "Well, we can't all be physicists."

Physicists: "That pocket protector is really *you*!"

Dogs: "Some people find drooling very attractive."

Podiatrists: "Too bad you couldn't be a *real* doctor."

Astronauts: "I hear NASA used to have really stringent requirements."

Hare Krishnas: "May you be reborn as someone less annoying."

Postal Workers: "Reading all those complicated zip codes would cause anyone to snap."

Fitness Instructors: "With all the problems facing the world today, I can see why it's important to have a tight butt."

Cowboys: "John Wayne . . . now there was a *real* cowboy!"

Models: "If I had your looks, I wouldn't think either."

Butchers: "Guess you must like the smell of blood, huh?"

Stockbrokers: "Don't feel bad. It's your job to be greedy."

Policemen: "It must be tough, eating all those free donuts."

Insurance Agents: "Sure, my premiums are out of sight. But it's worth it to get that cheap pocket calendar from you every year."

Journalists: "I know that if you had the budget, you could be doing major news stories like Geraldo."

DUMB AS AN ODIE

Chased any parked cars lately?

When it comes to dumb, Odie is in a class by himself—a class for village idiots and problem droolers. He's so dumb, it took him three years to learn how to breathe. His IQ is so low, you can't test it; you have to dig for it. Of course, he was bred to be a working dog—specifically, a paperweight or a doorstop. Maybe you know someone this stupid? If so, tell them to come in out of the rain. Then tell them a few more things:

You're a person of rare intelligence. It's rare when you show any.

You're smarter than you look. But then, you'd *have* to be!

If space aliens captured you, they'd report no intelligent life on Earth!

I'd like to pick your brain, but I don't have tweezers that small.

Lifestyles of the Really Stupid?
...u been thinking?

...a with a chicken and got the
...cluck!

...he dictionary, and there was a

...ience, and they made an early

Can I borrow your brain? You're obviously not using it!

You're a mental midget. When it comes to smarts, you come up short.

You'd have to be twice as smart just to be a half-wit.

If ignorance is bliss, you should be the world's happiest person.

You'll never have a mental breakdown. There are no moving parts up there.

Were you always this stupid, or is it just since your lobotomy?

I've seen scarecrows with more brains than you.

Have you ever considered a career as a crash dummy?

You can't count to twenty without taking your shoes off.

Your SAT scores will definitely get you into college. Barber college.

You'd have to study just to be stupid.

You're so dumb, you flunked recess!

Your parents must have lots of brains, because they didn't give any to you!

You'll never lose your mind. You can't lose what you never had.

Leonard Nimoy called. He wants to go in search of your brain!

Were you born stupid, or did you grow that way?

A word to the wise. Oh well, guess that leaves you out.

What you lack in intelligence, you make up for in stupidity.

Your brain must be in perfect shape. After all, it's never been used!

Your brain is like the Abominable Snowman. Neither one has ever been found!

You're so boneheaded, you make Odie look like a Rhodes Scholar.

You've got a baby face ... and a brain to match!

It never fails. The bigger the hair, the smaller the brain.

Your problem is psychonomadic. Your mind wanders.

Don't worry if your mind wanders. It's too weak to get very far.

If you were smarter, you'd know how dumb you are.

Heard you got a zit on your butt, and the doctors were worried because it was so close to your brain.

They're going to give you a new brain just as soon as the monkey dies.

They can't measure your intelligence. The scale won't go that low.

You're so dumb ...

   ... you think serial killers put poison in people's corn flakes!

   ... you think a baby-sitter sits on babies!

   ... you'd go to a garage sale to buy a garage!

   ... you think a monkey wrench is something you use to fix a monkey!

   ... you'd sleep with the windows open in a submarine!

... you'd try to fish off the back of a rowing machine!

... a mind reader would only charge you half-price!

... you'd pull an all-nighter studying for a blood test!

... you'd try to pitch horseshoes without taking them off the horse!

... you think a flower pot is used to cook flowers!

... you think a restaurant is a place you go to rest!

... you'd take little bars of soap to a baby shower!

... you think toothpaste is for loose teeth!

... you think a tailor is a guy who makes tails!

... you'd cut off your arms to wear a sleeveless shirt!

... you think a flea market is a place that sells fleas!

ODIE'S TOP TEN CONFUSED CLICHES

10. In one nostril and out the other
9. Caught with his head in the cookie jar
8. All dressed up and no place to drool
7. Cold hands, warm liver
6. I'll be a donkey's uncle
5. His breath is worse than his bite
4. Between a rock and a hard-boiled egg
3. A new leash on life
2. Keep a stiff rubber lip
1. Two tongues are better than one

TOP TEN REASONS WHY ODIE CAN'T READ

10. Had a tough time just learning to breathe
9. Illiterate Marmaduke a bad influence
8. Didn't want to learn from teacher; just wanted to lick her face
7. Poor curriculum: too much *Beowulf*, not enough "Huckleberry Hound"
6. Was sick that day
5. Paper-training gave him a low opinion of print matter
4. Television
3. Came from one of those "jock" pet shops
2. Tough to decipher drool-soaked pages
1. Three words: just plain stupid!

6 Best uses for an Odie

STEP STOOL

TV ANTENNA

SCAPEGOAT

DISHWASHER

TABLE LEG

PAPERWEIGHT

81

OUT TO LUNCH

My kingdom for a fruitcake!

Are you one donut shy of a dozen? Are there
beans in your pod? Have your enchiladas lost their
chili? Do you know what I'm saying? I'm saying you're
BANANAS! CRACKERS! NUTS! You're not just nutty
as a fruitcake . . . you're nuttier than a squirrel's break-
fast! I'd take you out to lunch, but you already are.

Am I driving you crazy? (A short drive, no doubt.)
Well, don't lose it. You're not alone. Lunacy loves company. It takes one to know one. Do you know what I'm
saying? I'm saying that *I'm* bonkers, too! That's right.
Insanity is contagious and I caught it from you. I'm off
my rocker! Out of my tree! Over the edge! I'm fishing
without bait with only one oar in the water. In fact, I've
lost my marbles, flipped my lid, gone around the bend
and clear off the deep end!

But I'm still not as mental as you. On the highway of
life, you're a stalled vehicle. Your battery's dead and
your brain's stuck in neutral. They're gonna have to
tow you to the loony bin. If you were a building, you'd
be condemned. There are bats in your belfry, termites
in your attic, and a leak in your think tank. And to top
it off, your elevator doesn't go to the penthouse.

So what's the deal? Why aren't you playing with a

any games with-
tight? Whatever
. Don't deny it.
re not). Take it

RFIELD IS

and Odie as Si-

9. ~~Convinced he's being stalked by~~ a giant pickle
8. Develops sudden interest in aerobics
7. Weeps uncontrollably every time Wile E. Coyote falls off cliff
6. Thinks Jon is a snappy dresser
5. Can name all the members of the Mormon Tabernacle Choir
4. Will only answer to the name "Clarence"
3. Compulsively seeks out insurance salesmen
2. Sends Snoopy fan mail
1. Skips dessert

DARTS TO THE HEART

It was love at first sight. Then I took a second look!

Love makes the world go 'round. Unfortunately, it also makes the heart ache, the stomach turn, and the brain go nuts. First you break up, then you throw up, then you crack up. Next thing you know, you're hard up and on a blind date, wishing you were blind. That's right. You've come full circle and are once more part of the dating scene. And it's a jungle out there. Actually, it's more like a kennel. Ever feel like your date should be wearing a flea collar? Anyway, the heart of the matter is this: in the topsy-turvy world of dating, where kissing can turn to dissing in the wink of an eye (especially if you're caught winking at the wrong person), it pays to have a blistering tongue to go along with your burning lips. Here are your darts. Remember to aim for the heart.

Blowing off losers

I can't go out with you for medical reasons. You make me sick.

Sorry, I don't date lower life-forms.

Make my day. Ask someone else out tonight.

That pick-up line's so lame it needs crutches.

I can't date you yet. I still have standards.

I'd consider going out with you, but I'm still in my right mind.

You're the last of the red-hot losers.

You think you're hot stuff, but your sizzle has fizzled.

If they can send a man to the moon, why don't they send you?

Dumping on your dates

Dating you proves one thing: nightmares *can* come true!

You've made this a date I won't forget ... no matter how hard I try.

You might be great in history, but you're lousy on dates.

Kiss you? I'd rather kiss an orangutan with a cold sore.

I know why they call this a "blind date." Because now that I've seen you, I wish I were blind.

Let's not see each other for a while. Like the rest of our lives.

I really enjoyed myself. Too bad I didn't enjoy you.

We have a pretty weird relationship. I'm pretty and you're weird.

You're a man of the nineties. Naturally, I'm referring to your IQ.

Are you wearing musk or muskrat?

Let's go dutch. You pay; I'll wear wooden shoes.

Kiss you? I'd rather plant one on a porcupine's posterior!

Ragging on other people and their dates

You haven't had a date in so long, they should feature you on *America's Most Unwanted*.

You're like disposable diapers . . . always getting dumped.

I heard your dates like to kiss you . . . kiss you off!

You've been stood up more times than a bowling pin.

You've been shot down so many times you should wear a parachute.

I hear you had a hot 'n' heavy date. You were hot and your date was heavy.

The only thing worse than no dates are *your* dates.

Your date has a nice mustache. How long has she had it?

Your date was so ugly, she had to wear a paper bag when she used the phone.

I heard there was a girl who liked you, but she got professional help.

The computer found your perfect date. But the zoo won't let her out!

One look at your date tells me she has a good personality.

You've dated some real dogs. And the women weren't too attractive, either!

All your dates are the same . . . inflatable!

Your date looks familiar. Didn't she have the title role in *Alien*?

What time does your date have to be back in the sty?

Your date has nice hair. Too bad it's growing on her back.

I heard you almost had a date, but she chewed off her leg and escaped.

Did you get a goodnight kiss, or did you just shake her paw?

Of course you got to first base. And I'm Jose Canseco.

If you swept her off her feet, you must have used a broom the size of Alaska!

To date you a girl has to be double D: desperate and deranged!

Is that your date, or did your brother get a new dress?

Your date was so ugly that instead of the "ladies room," she went to the "creatures room!"

Your last date buried the needle on the "Beast-ometer."

Your dates don't wear much. Usually, just a flea collar.

Hey, Beastmaster! Go smooch a pooch!

To shoot your date, Cupid would need an elephant gun!

Your date is dark and handsome. When it's dark, he's handsome.

Your date's a real hunk. A hunk of what is anybody's guess!

Know what dating all those jocks makes you? A big athletic supporter!

Your date doesn't cut the mustard. But he sure cuts the cheese!

You don't attract guys like crazy. You attract crazy guys.

Snappy comebacks

"What would you say if I asked you out?"
"Nothing. I can't talk and gag at the same time."

"What are you doing Friday night?"
"Trying to forget you just asked me that."

"I'd have to be desperate *and* insane to go out with you."
"So when should I pick you up?"

"I have a big date tonight."
"How big is she?"

"What's he got that I haven't?"
"You want it alphabetically?"

"Haven't we met?"

"In *your* dreams and *my* nightmares."

Liz: I'm single, not desperate.

Sorry, I don't date outside my species.

Will you hand me that large mallet?

I'd rather shave my head with a chain saw!

No, it's too dangerous. I might yawn myself to
death.

Sure, then I'll donate my life's savings to gypsies.

TOP TEN EXCUSES FOR BREAKING A DATE

10. "Don't know how I forgot this engagement at Buckingham Palace."
9. "My cousin really needs my kidney."
8. "I'd let you talk to the space aliens, but for some reason they can only communicate with me."
7. "It's a hair thing. I know you'll understand."
6. "That must have been one of my other personalities."
5. "Everything before the accident is a blank."
4. "I just remembered—I'm married."
3. "I know it's last-minute, but I've decided to change my sex."
2. "Sorry, I had you confused with someone attractive."
1. "I'm probably not contagious, but ..."

JON ARBUCKLE'S TOP TEN PICK-UP LINES

10. "Excuse me, have you seen my Nobel Prize around here anywhere?"
9. "I'm still into macrame. How about you?"
8. "You look like a woman with low standards."
7. "You've certainly got the figure for that dumpy cashier's outfit."
6. "When I saw you, I lost control of all my bodily functions."
5. "Ever been hit on by a cartoon character?"
4. "Are you as lonely and depressed as I am?"
3. "I have very few communicable diseases."
2. "Please. I'm begging you."
1. "Uh ... uh ... um ... duh ... cough ..."

ALLITERATIVE AFFRONTS

Silly slams on stupid subjects

When cut-ups want to cut down something, they often use a rhetorical device called "alliteration" to jazz up their jive. If you don't know what alliteration is, you'll probably figure it out by the end of this chapter. If it doesn't dawn on you, do not dillydally, but go directly to a dictionary, you ditzy dim-witted dipstick. Anyway, from A to Z, these are a few of my least favorite fings (What? You never heard of poetic license?):

A: airheaded aerobicizing Arbuckles
B: bad bowser breath
C: corny clumsy cartoonists
D: dippy dopey dogs
E: exhausting excruciating exercise
F: foul fertilized farms
G: gross gargantuan goiters
H: humongous hacked-up hairballs
I: irritable illiterate insomniacs
J: jolly jowly joggers
K: cute conniving kittens
L: lame leftover liver
M: malicious malodorous mice
N: noisy nosy neighbors

O: obese off-key opera singers

P: namby-pamby party poopers

Q: quiche-eatin' Quasimodo-lookin' Quakers (Got a hunch I'm gonna get in dutch with certain Pennsylvanians over this one.)

R: wrinkled rancid raisins

S: spewing spastic spiders

T: tyrannical test-toting teachers

U: ugly uncoordinated unicyclists

V: vicious vindictive veterinarians

W: Winnie the Pooh underwear-wearin' wimps

X: X-words? . . . Get real! In fact, if you can come up with three, I'll eat a wrinkled rancid raisin!

Y: yammering yellowbellied yahoos

Z: zonked-out zit-faced zombies

COTTON-PICKIN' PUT-DOWNS
... from down in the boondocks

Kiss my grits, Possum Breath!

Hornswoggled in Hooterville? Well, don't let no dadburn ornery varmint git your goat. If'n some rude-rube-bubbleheaded Bubba is aimin' for a maimin', then you give 'em a hurtin' for certain. (Don't you just love this here talk?) Yep, when in the boondocks, do as the boondockers do.

You're lower than a snake's belly in a wagon rut.

You're stankier than a skunk's armpit.

You smell like an acre of wet dogs.

You're so cheap, you squeeze a dollar till the eagle hollers.

Your cookin' could gag a maggot.

You're as ornery as a hungry goat with a toothache.

You're as worthless as a milk pail under a bull.

You got the IQ of a turnip.

Your brain's punier than a gnat's whisker.

If brains were leather, you couldn't saddle a flea.

You couldn't track a three-legged cow in four feet of snow.

You look like you've been whupped with the ugly stick.

You're uglier than a mud fence.

You look like ninety miles of bad road.

Your face is so freckled it looks like you swallowed a dollar and broke out in pennies.

You're so bucktoothed, you could eat corn through a picket fence.

You're so crooked, you could hide behind a corkscrew.

You're as slippery as a wet fish.

You're like a blister. You don't show up till the work is done.

Let's play horse. I'll be the front end; you just be yourself.

GARFIELD'S TOP TEN CORNIEST COUNTRY TUNES

10. Mama Sang Bass, Daddy Had Worms
 9. Lipstick on Your Flea Collar, Cheatin' on Your Mind
 8. I Burp As Much In Texas As I Did In Tennessee
 7. Call Me A Hairball Tomorrow, But Feed Me Tonight
 6. Bubba Shot the Litterbox
 5. Odie from Muskogee
 4. Mamas Don't Let Your Kittens Grow Up To Be Professional Wrestlers
 3. Walk Softly On This Tail Of Mine
 2. You Used To Be My Chew Toy, But I Used To Have Real Teeth
 1. Honky-Tonk Tabby (Gettin' Old . . . Feelin' Flabby)

GARFIELD'S TOP TEN FAVORITE THINGS TO DO ON THE ARBUCKLE FARM

10. Put down Roy Clark and the whole *Hee Haw* gang
9. Shake up the animals with some frank talk about the food chain
8. Give Odie a good threshing
7. Plant some chickens
6. Fertilize Doc Boy's overalls
5. Baste the hogs
4. Party till the cows come home, then party with the cows
3. Sleep
2. Harvest the fridge
1. Leave

HIGHBROW BROWBEATING
or
Taunting your adversary while flaunting your vocabulary

"Beware! Big words ahead!"

I don't know about you, but I'm tired of the same old insulting names. "Geek," "dork," "dweeb" ... **BORING**! Name-calling needn't be humdrum; it can also be educational—and fun, of course. I mean, why settle for a big mouth when you can also have a large vocabulary?! Inasmuch, here are some epithets (that's a fancy word for "names") guaranteed to make you sound like you've attended a prestigious boarding school—in the 19th century, no less. Please note that I've been kind enough to provide lowbrow definitions for all you lazy *ignoramuses* (doofuses) who have conveniently misplaced your dictionaries.

muckworm (cheapskate)
guttersnipe (scumbucket)
chucklehead (dunce)
lickspittle (suck-up)
milksop (sissy)
poltroon (chicken)
smellfungus (case-buster)
gasbag (braggart)
plug-ugly (punk)
lummox (oaf)
popinjay (dandy)
fishwife (shrew)
scalawag (rascal)
scaramouch (buffoon)
toady (yes-man)
blatherskite (babbler)
nincompoop (fool)
jackanapes (monkey)
slugabed (lazybones)
blunderbuss (klutz)
humbug (phony)
jackal (henchman)
yokel (bumpkin)
quidnunc (gossip)
sneaksby (weasel)
cur (mongrel)
flibbertigibbet (birdbrain)

PUTTING DOWN THE DOG

*In the weenie of life, dogs are the
animal by-products*

Friends, dogcatchers, countrymen, lend me your ears. I come to bury Rover, not to praise him. I mean, why waste my breath talking about something with the IQ of an artichoke? Speaking of breath ... did you know that dog breath actually killed a guy in Utah? Anyway, as far as I'm concerned, the only good dog is a hot dog! Of course, if you choose not to let stinking dogs lie, here's your very own canine cap-down starter kit. So don't just stand there. Flog the dog!

Your dog is so dumb, he once tried to bury a trombone.
Your dog is so slow, he fetches yesterday's newspaper.
Your dog can't walk and drool at the same time.
That's not a dog. That's a walking flea farm.
Your dog is uglier than a tarantula on a bad hair day.
Your pooch is so ugly, he can't even get a date with a fire hydrant.
I've seen better looking dogs scraped off the highway!
Is that your dog or a barking salami?
That yappy mutt has more bark than a redwood.
Your dog doesn't need a muzzle. He needs a laryngectomy!
The only trick your dog can do is "play stupid."

113

WHAT HUMANS SEE	WHAT CATS SEE

Your dog couldn't find a bone in a butcher's shop.

Your dog is so lazy, he only chases parked cars.

Life's a bowl of cherries, and dogs are the pits.

I'm not prejudiced. I hate *all* dogs!

Your dog's breath could stun a skunk.

Your dog has a face even a flea couldn't love.

I'd say your dog looks like a warthog, but I don't want
 to insult the warthog.

What do you feed a dog like yours? Purina Rat Chow?

Your dog's a rare breed: 100% ugly!

That's not a dog. That's a furry maggot.

That mangy mutt's about as cute as carpet stains.

114

Your dog is such a weenie that cats chase *him*!

Your dog's so scrawny, he could lie under a clothesline and not get sunburned.

If that hound were any lazier, he'd slip into a coma.

Your dog's so decrepit, the only thing he does fast is get tired.

I hate every bone in your dog's body. And I'm not real fond of his muscles, either!

Why don't you trade your dog for something smarter? Like a rock.

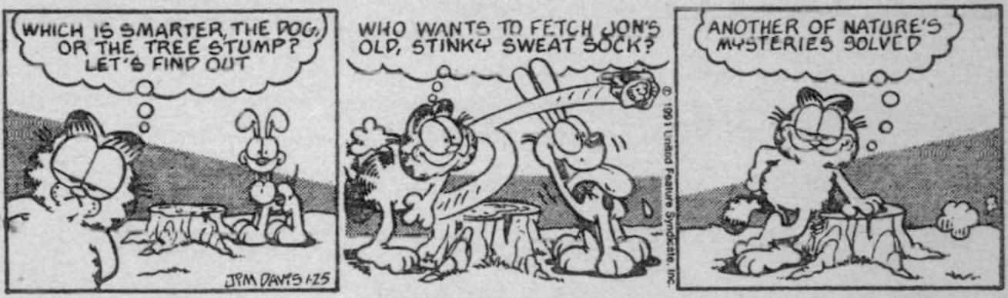

WHICH IS SMARTER, THE DOG, OR THE TREE STUMP? LET'S FIND OUT
WHO WANTS TO FETCH JON'S OLD, STINKY SWEAT SOCK?
ANOTHER OF NATURE'S MYSTERIES SOLVED

With a dog like that, you'll always have a doorstop.

The difference between your dog and an eggplant is about three IQ points!

When they were passing out brains, your dog thought they said "trains," so he got out of the way!

Your dog's so stupid, he chases bones and buries cars!

Nice dog. Were they all out of cute ones?

What do you call that big ugly mutt . . . Dogzilla?!

Your dog's so mean, his own shadow won't keep him company.

That's not a dog. That's a hairball with a tail.

The last time I saw something that looked like your dog, I called an exterminator.

Your dog is so disgusting even the garbage man won't pick him up.

Why don't you take that stinking dog to a laundro-mutt?

Your dog's breath is worse than his bite.

They could never use your dog for medical experiments. Even germs won't touch him.

CATS' TOP TEN DEMEANING NAMES FOR DOGS

10. Pound scum
 9. Sniveling face-lickers
 8. Four-legged flea farms
 7. Drool fools
 6. Leash monkeys
 5. Pack-happy cat molesters
 4. Toilet-lappers
 3. Hydrant Harrys
 2. Road rugs
 1. Odies

TOP TEN REASONS DOGS ARE
EXPELLED FROM OBEDIENCE SCHOOL

10. Drinking from the faculty toilet
 9. Never turning in homework. Always claiming owner ate it.
 8. Licking themselves during the Pledge of Allegiance
 7. Wearing "Cats Suck" T-shirts in direct violation of school dress code
 6. Mooning passing cars
 5. Playing hooky when they should be playing dead
 4. Cutting in linc at the hydrant during "tinkle time"
 3. Sticking nose where it doesn't belong
 2. Hiding crib notes on back of flea collar
 1. Ripping out throat of trainer

PROFESSOR GARFIELD'S

NATURAL HISTORY OF DOGS

PROTO-DOG

A BRAINLESS SLIME DWELLER.

**DOGOSAUR
12 MILLION B.C.**

HAD THE MISFORTUNE TO LIVE BEFORE TREES AND FIRE HYDRANTS HAD EVOLVED; SOON EXTINCT.

**CRO-MAGNON DOG
10,000 B.C.**

DOMESTICATED BUT STILL NOT HOUSEBROKEN.

**WOOD-BURNING DOG
CA. 1850**

ANOTHER MISTAKE.

MODERN DOG

AS YOU CAN SEE, NOT A LOT OF PROGRESS.

BIRTHDAY BASHING

Hey, Prune Face! Your birthday suit could use some starch!

We all know it's not polite to make fun of a person's age; however, it is a lot of fun. But it can also be dangerous. (Those canes really smart!) So if *you* want to live to be a ripe old age, use these age slams with caution:

I'm not saying you're old, but who else . . .

   . . . has wrinkles on their teeth?

   . . . sprinkles tenderizer on their applesauce?

   . . . had a pterodactyl for a pet?

   . . . knew Bigfoot when he wore booties?

   . . . remembers when Baskin-Robbins only had two flavors?

   . . . wears steel-belted support hose?

   . . . has hieroglyphics on their birth certificate?

   . . . knew Alexander the Great when he was just mediocre?

... knew Sleeping Beauty when she was an ugly insomniac?

What do you take in your coffee? Cream, sugar, or formaldehyde?

Mind if I play connect-the-dots on your liver spots?

You look like a million. That's an estimate, not a compliment.

You're so old, they had to carbon-date you!

Tell me, Gramps. What was it like working on the pyramids?

If you were a car, it'd be time to roll back your odometer.

Do you dye your hair, or is it naturally blue?

Your teeth are like the stars. They come out at night.

Your smile should be bronzed. So take out your teeth and let's do it!

Hey, Trifocal Face! Read any good eye charts lately?

You've got so many varicose veins, your body could double as a road map.

It looks like the Wrinkle Fairy tap-danced on your face.

You have a lot of funny lines. Too bad they're all on your face.

I've seen stale raisins with less wrinkles.

Know how people your age celebrate a birthday? Very carefully!

Is that your cake or a three-alarm fire?

The older people get, the more you should respect them. And I respect you more than anyone I know!

I'd never make fun of your age. You might whack me with your cane!

I'll say one thing for you. You don't wheeze much for a geezer.

Hey, Fossil Face! You don't need a plastic surgeon. You need an archeologist!

Compared to you, Methuselah died young!

Are there always vultures circling this house?

I'm ready to light the candles on your cake. Hand me the blowtorch.

You know you're getting old when . . .

    . . . you go to an antique auction and three people
        bid on you!
    . . . the only hair you can grow is in your nose!
    . . . you tear a rotator cuff waving goodbye!
    . . . your toupee develops a receding hairline!
    . . . they ask to check your bags and you're not
        carrying luggage!
    . . . someone tells you your pantyhose are wrinkled
        and you're not wearing any!
    . . . your brain says, "Go for it!" and your body says,
        "Not now, I'm busy breathing."
    . . . you get winded on escalators!
    . . . you sprain your wrist flossing!
    . . . you'd rather gawk at Miss Piggy than Miss Oc-
        tober!
    . . . your favorite cartoon is *Bullwrinkle*!

NONVERBAL JABS

Why say it when you can display it?

With put-downs, sometimes less is more. A look, a gesture, or even a well-played practical joke can often pack more wallop than mere words.

Trust me—looks can kill. (Have you seen Jon first thing in the morning?) A look can convey feelings ranging from mild disdain to outright mockery:

The Sneer:

This look provides just the right mixture of arrogance and contempt. Lets the world know that *you* are cool, while virtually everyone else is something you scrape off your shoe. A must for teenagers.

The Eyeball Roll:

Indicates that some thickheaded, exasperating lower life-form is wasting your valuable time, but you have too much class to raise a stink about it. Very useful when traveling abroad.

The Brick Face:

This is a look of total indifference that says that you are perfectly aware of what's happening around you, but are too important to show the slightest interest in such trivia. Good expression to use on dogs, singing telegrams, special prosecutors.

The Crushing Smile:

Used primarily when you are being introduced, this smile puts people in their place by saying, "The pleasure is all yours. Now, why don't you get back on the buffet with the other vegetables?"

Gestures often speak louder than words. Clasping your hands together means you are serious. Clasping them around someone else's throat means you are very serious. You can also get an edge in conversation by poking the other person in the chest, preferably with a cattle prod. Other ways to insult and intimidate people include staring until they look away, standing on their toes, and sticking your chewing gum to their forehead.

And, of course, never overlook the time-honored tradition of making faces. Two simple, but effective moves are sticking your tongue out (the farther, the better) or the raspberry (the wetter, the better).

Practical jokes are often the most impractical form of put-downs. They can require a large investment of time and thought. But the pay-off can be equally great. And sometimes a verbal assault just isn't enough. You gotta get physical. You gotta take matters into your own paws. Watch and learn. A picture's worth a thousand words.

LIFE IN THE FAT LANE

Seen your feet lately?

I've trashed Odie and dumped on Jon so I guess it's time to sling a little mud my own way. But that's okay. I can dish it out and I can take it. It takes a big man—or in my case, a fat cat—to do that. Not that I'm really overweight; actually, I'm just undertall. Besides, it beats being skinny and looking like you've been pulled through a keyhole. But for the sake of mirth at the expense of girth (and because I need another chapter to round out this book), let's stop chewing the fat and start poking fun at it.

You know you're getting fat when . . .

    . . . your new house is a blimp hangar!

    . . . waiters bring you the dessert menu first!

    . . . they feed you with a harpoon!

    . . . you start sweating butter!

    . . . you hurt the bathtub!

YOU KNOW YOU'RE GETTING **FAT** WHEN...

EVERY TIME YOU GO TO
THE BEACH, THE TIDE
COMES IN

SOMEONE TRIES TO CLIMB
YOUR NORTH SLOPE

YOU HAVE THIS TREMENDOUS
URGE TO GRAZE

THE PHONE COMPANY GIVES
YOU YOUR OWN AREA CODE

YOUR PICTURE IS POSTED IN
"ALL-YOU-CAN-EAT" RESTAURANTS

WARNING!

NASA ORBITS A SATELLITE
AROUND YOU

... you can "pinch an inch" on your forehead!

... even your mom starts calling you "Moby"!

... you think Garfield is in pretty good shape!

Are we having an eclipse, or is that just your gut blotting out the sun?

Excuse me, sir. When's the baby due?

Are you sure you're full? There's still a little left in your trough.

You're not a fat broad. You're a woman of size.

What are you gonna be when you grow up? A physical fatness instructor?

Hey, Jelly Belly! Where's *Mrs.* Claus?

You were such a fat baby, the stork couldn't deliver you. They had to get a crane.

Hey, Tubbo! Don't cry over spilt milk. Get down there and lap it up!

You don't need to go on a diet. You need to go on a hunger strike!

The only thing bigger than your stomach is your appetite.

You don't just shovel it in. You *bulldoze* it in!

You don't need a bib. You need a tarp!

I know I said, "Dive right in," but I didn't mean it literally!

Hey, Jaws! Are you ever coming up for air?

Hey, Hoover! Turn off the vacuum!

Is that your stomach, or did you swallow a globe?

You're a light eater. As soon as it gets light, you start
 eating.

You eat like a bird. Larry Bird.

We have enough food to feed an army. Or we can just
 feed *you*!

What you lack in brain cells, you make up for in fat
 cells.

Hey, Lard Gut! That's one spare tire that'll never go
 flat!

Your heart's in the right place. However, your stomach
 is hanging down by your knees.

You're living proof of the theory "survival of the
 fattest."

Is that your shadow, or is there a street gang following
 you?

Shall we chew the fat? Or do you just want to swallow
 it whole?

Hey, Porky! If I slopped your trough, would you be in
 hog heaven? (Oink once for yes.)

You have a memory like an elephant. And a figure like
 one, too.

Is that your underwear on the clothesline or a parachute?

That's a whale of a tail you've got there, Blubber Butt!

You've got a caboose as big as a moose!

With a bubblebutt like yours, the problem is definitely in the jeans.

I'll say one thing for you. You're obviously well reared.

Hey, Hippo Hips! Bust any toilet seats lately?

You're such a rumpasaurus, when you start to sit down, the chairs beg for mercy!

You're so fat . . .

   . . . people exercise by running laps around you!

   . . . the government wants to make you a state!

   . . . I need double-vision to see you!

   . . . you were born with a silver shovel in your mouth!

   . . . when you were a baby, your first word was "Oink"!

   . . . your favorite food is fifths!

   . . . your shoes smile when you take them off!

   . . . when you roll over, it registers on the Richter scale!

GARFIELD'S TOP TEN EUPHEMISMS FOR "FAT"

10. "Corporally well-endowed"
 9. "Sofa-bodied"
 8. "Santa-waisted"
 7. "Seam-testing"
 6. "Ebertine"
 5. "Up-sized petite"
 4. "Sun-blotting"
 3. "Experiencing a cell surplus"
 2. "Dinner-friendly"
 1. "Orson-esque"

Garfield impressions

BEACHED WHALE

BLIMP

SMALL PLANET

COMATOSE HIPPO

MONTANA

OVERSTUFFED SOFA

PARTING SHOTS

Good-bye. The pleasure was all yours

Parting is such sweet sorrow—unless, of course, you're saying good-bye to your dentist; then it's just sweet. It can also be cool. A smart-aleck adios to an amigo can be the verbal equivalent of a secret handshake, a bonding thing between buddies. In my case, Odie licks me and I give him the ol' "bon voyage boot." But, alas, my soft side is showing. I'd better go before I get too choked up. See ya in the funny pages, Litterbox Breath!

It won't be the same around here without you. It'll be better.

There's a bus leaving at three. Be under it!

I hate to leave, but my doctor says boredom is bad for me.

Have a nice day someplace else.

Leave now, while I can still act like I care.

How can I miss you if you won't go away?

Take a hike ... preferably to the Bermuda Triangle.

Let me show you the door. On second thought, let me show you the upstairs window.

The fun's just starting, so you must be going.

So long. Do forget to write.

I'll treasure every moment that you're gone.

Don't ever change. I want to forget you just the way you are.

I'll miss you like I'll miss poison ivy.

You better go. I think I hear your mommy calling you.

Words can't describe how I feel about you leaving. So I'll just applaud.

Good-bye! Good luck! Good riddance!

Let's go someplace where we can each be alone.

Thanks for leaving. Feel free to do it anytime.

So long. It was everything I dreaded it would be.

Are you leaving? I hadn't noticed you were here.

Don't tell me you're leaving. Unless you're not coming back.

Let's not do this again and say we did.

I hate saying "good-bye," but in your case I'll do it gladly.

Whenever you're in the neighborhood, I won't be home.

Isn't it time you were annoying someone else?

Before you leave, I just want to say those three little words: "Don't come back."

Good-bye. We're so sad you could come.

Good night. Or it will be as soon as you leave.

I'd love to help you out. Which way did you come in?

Take your face to outer space!

Go sleep face-down on a bed of nails!

Make like a tree and leave!
Make like a dog and get lost!

Make like a tire and hit the road!
Make like a bee and buzz off!
Make like a banana and split!
Make like the wind and blow!
Make like E.T. and go home!
Make like dandruff and flake off!

Adios, Burrito Breath!

Sayonara, Sushi Brain!
Ciao, Pizza Face!
Au revoir, Escargot Tongue!
Arrivederci, Meatball Head!
Cheerio, Crumpet Nose!
Hasta la pasta, Linguine Lips!
Get thee to a cannery, Fish Face!
See you soon, you big maroon!
Vamoose, you silly goose!
Get out of town by sundown, clown!
Get a job, slob!
So long, King Kong!

"See you later, alligator."
"After awhile, Gomer Pyle."

"See you later."
"Not if I see you first."

CATS ALWAYS HAVE TO
HAVE THE LAST LAUGH

HA! HA! HA! HA!
HA! HA! HA! HA!
HA

GARFIELD

and the gang

Published by Ballantine Books.

Call toll free 1-800-793-BOOK (2665) to order by phone and use your major credit card. Or use this coupon to order by mail.

__GARFIELD AT LARGE	345-32013-1	$6.95
__GARFIELD GAINS WEIGHT	345-32008-5	$6.95
__GARFIELD BIGGER THAN LIFE	345-32007-7	$8.95
__GARFIELD TAKES THE CAKE	345-32009-3	$6.95
__GARFIELD EATS HIS HEART OUT	345-32018-2	$6.95
__GARFIELD SITS AROUND THE HOUSE	345-32011-5	$6.95
__GARFIELD LOSES HIS FEET	345-31805-6	$6.95
__GARFIELD MAKES IT BIG	345-31928-1	$6.95
__GARFIELD ROLLS ON	345-32634-2	$6.95
__GARFIELD WORLDWIDE	345-35158-4	$6.95
__GARFIELD KEEPS HIS CHINS UP	345-37959-4	$6.95
__GARFIELD PULLS HIS WEIGHT	345-38666-3	$6.95

GARFIELD AT HIS SUNDAY BEST!

__THE GARFIELD TREASURY	345-32106-5	$12.50
__THE SECOND GARFIELD TREASURY	345-33276-6	$12.00
__THE THIRD GARFIELD TREASURY	345-32635-0	$12.00
__THE FIFTH GARFIELD TREASURY	345-36268-3	$12.00
__THE SEVENTH GARFIELD TREASURY	345-38427-X	$10.95

Name_____

Address_____

City_____State_____Zip _____

Please send me the BALLANTINE BOOKS I have checked above.

I am enclosing	$_____
plus	
Postage & handling*	$_____
Sales tax (where applicable)	$_____
Total amount enclosed	$_____

*Add $4 for the first book and $1 for each additional book.

Send check or money order (no cash or CODs) to:
Ballantine Mail Sales, 400 Hahn Road, Westminster, MD 21157.

Prices and numbers subject to change without notice.
Valid in the U.S. only.

All orders subject to availability.   DAVIS